# MASTERING THE MIND-BODY CONNECTION

## RALPH CISSNE



For more visit willofgolf.com

ISBN 978-0-9998537-9-5

morganroad.com

Design & Production: Wendy Saade
10spacedesign.com

Cover Photograph:
Ocean Trails, Rancho Palos Verdes, California

Yoga Photography: Diana Postik

Yoga Postures: Richelle Kristi Fritzl

# MASTERING THE MIND-BODY CONNECTION

## RALPH CISSNE

Dedicated to the memory
of Myra A. Cissne.
Loving mother. True friend.

When a golfer turns their
attention away from the objective
all they see are obstacles.

# TABLE OF CONTENTS

Reflect on how your game
has improved. Notice how you
feel when you focus on what you
have created. Hold that thought.

# INTRODUCTION

Excellent instruction. Confidence. Practice. Fitted equipment. These are all essential components for playing your best, but there is another factor that is equally important. Every great golfer, regardless of age, possesses the presence of mind and the will to succeed. Some may be born with these advantages, but they are clearly skills to be learned.

The Will of Golf program is based on a lifetime of loving the game, the great characters I've known, and exploring the mind-body connection. These lessons will empower you to transform your mental and physical approach. Participation in this process can take you anywhere you want to go. You will improve your self-confidence by learning how to:

- *Flexibility:* Increase your range of motion and power.
- *Balance:* Use breathwork to relax and focus your attention.
- *Focus:* Transform your attitude into strategic thinking.
- *Results:* Create, at will, the shots you choose.

Perhaps the most significant revelation is recognizing the benefits of lightening up and *playing* golf. I was fortunate to learn the game surrounded by talented players who challenged me. Mastering the moment requires neither being serious nor foolish. You only need to be aware of where you are and what you want. This book presents techniques to release negative conditioning and realize the results you choose. Yoga postures increase your strength and flexibility while improving your ability to relax and focus effortlessly. This is an opportunity to experience an improved sense of effectiveness, which you can recreate *at will* on and off the course. We are here to enjoy life, and life is infinitely more enjoyable when you are playing well.

**MY RESULTS:** After publication of the original Will of Golf program in 2001, and many years competing against better players, in 2003 I won our Club Championship and was runner up in our President's Cup match play (giving the 14-index winner 9 shots). My index dropped to zero for a healthy stretch. In the following ten years I won our Senior Club Championship (age 50+) eight times and finished in the top ten of the Los Angeles Senior Amateur Championship five times. My game improved and so will yours.

Most of our shots are taken
from inside 100 yards. Dedicate at least
half your practice to improving your
short game, chipping and putting.
Sure way to lower your scores.

# LESSON 1: SELF-RELIANCE

A wise woman once told me: "All we have in life are moments, so make the most of them as they come along." The game of golf provides countless opportunities to be in the moment and explore the power of what's happening now. Golf is the ultimate test of your character, creativity and will.

As a golfer, when you are uncertain, when you turn your attention away from the objective, all you will see are obstacles. Fear creates stress and virtually assures your failure. Environmental stress stunts growth. At the cellular level, the will to survive is a biological imperative. Stress stimulates the adrenal glands, which causes your heart to pump blood to extremities. In a moment, the blood vessels in your brain constrict. Biologically, you are not prepared to think. You are prepared to fight or flee. In certain situations, an adrenaline rush may be helpful, but not on the golf course.

Every second four billion nerve impulses assault your brain. Only 2,000 of these impulses are conscious, the rest are relegated to the subconscious. Your mind is an extraordinarily busy place. When you practice something, when you master a task, it becomes automatic. The key is to consistently focus on the results you choose and to balance your energy. Listen to the world around you, how people speak about themselves. Most audio sensory input is negative. Be aware. Turn down the volume. Practice stillness.

Golf has always been about self-improvement. Few activities require such complete self-reliance. You must practice. You must learn to trust your swing. Your body knows what to do. It is your busy mind, ultimately, that gets in the way.

A round of golf is a succession of moments filled with opportunity. Consciously, move into each moment aware of the subtle transitions from moment to moment. In this willful state of mind, you create a chosen reality where all things are possible.

Change is inevitable. The universe
is a dynamic place. Go with the flow.
Embrace opportunity. Relax your grip.
Check your alignment.

# LESSON 2: CHOOSING YOUR TEACHERS

Throughout our lives we know many teachers. Family, friends and school provide a healthy dose of life experience and social conditioning. We learn the demands and rewards of relationships, career path, and parenting. Keeping up with what's happening in our crazed media-driven society, and the convergence of technology, it is easy to be overwhelmed with information.

## AVOID INFORMATION OVERLOAD

Golf is a magnificent obsession. Not everyone in your life may understand, but you do. Enjoy yourself as much as possible. If you want to improve, you must make some adjustments. To keep up with your perceived competition these adjustments often take the form of upgrading to the latest technology.

You may buy new equipment, read books and magazines, study videos and search the Internet looking for the latest hot topic. Have fun. Go for it. Be forewarned frustration inevitably arrives when you fail to practice a technique properly or when tips conflict. If your fundamentals are flawed, you feel it.

## PROFESSIONAL GOLF INSTRUCTION

Getting back to basics is always a good choice. A reasonable objective is to develop a simplified, repeatable swing that works for you. This is best done under the watchful eye of a professional. Ask players you respect to recommend an instructor. Take a lesson or two. If you like the teacher's approach and attitude, stick with them. The fundamentals of grip, posture, alignment, and tempo are essential. A good teacher will help you square the clubface and create power through dynamic leverage.

It's fun to explore tips and trends, but they have little value unless you invest the time to incorporate them into your game. Choose a teacher you trust. They will strengthen your fundamentals, encourage practice and help build your feel for the game.

"Your reality doesn't exist independent of your thoughts. You always cause the thought, which creates the action, which produces your results."

– Frank Natale

# LESSON 3: THE CHOICE TO THINK

Much of everyday conversation is negative and redundant. It's chatter really, to relieve a sense of anxiety or fill a moment of silence. Listen to your golf companions. Listen to your co-workers. Listen to yourself. Stop and think what you are saying.

On the course, "I can't hit a _________" or "I'm a terrible _________" are common refrains. The golf swing is basically a similar motion from club to club, so why would someone choose the point of view, "I can't hit a three iron." Why choose a negative outcome? Take a lesson. Work it out. Change your mind.

When you hear someone negating outcomes, have some fun by responding, "You're right. I don't recall you *ever* hitting a solid three iron. You're about 190 out, why not hit two wedges?" If you're not a wise guy, suggest that your friend take a lesson.

## MANIFESTING RESULTS

In the introduction of *Results: The Willingness to Create*, Frank Natale states: "Your reality is created by your thoughts. What you think, you create. Your reality doesn't exist independent of your thoughts. You always cause the thought, which creates the action, which produces your results."

You are the creator of your thoughts. The responsibility is yours. Be clear about this. Golf is synonymous with self-reliance and responsibility. So why choose a point of view that doesn't support the outcome of a shot well played? Why hold on to thought patterns and behavior that do not support who you choose to be?

Frank adds a note about creating results and seriousness, which is particularly appropriate for golfers: "Be playful. Get into your power. Don't confuse seriousness with effectiveness, discipline, understanding, thoughtfulness or compassion. They are not the same. Seriousness is valueless and disease oriented. Because you are now beginning to create your life the way you choose it to be, don't get serious. There is no point in getting results unless you enjoy them."

## TAKING RESPONSIBILITY NOW

The foundation of all negative thought is your most negative belief, which for most people is: **"I am not good enough."** This belief is reactive to former conditions or past experiences. Take a moment to reflect on how this reactive point of view may have impacted your game.

Consider events in your golf life or perhaps your relationships and career. For how many of these events are you willing to take responsibility? For how many of these events are you *unwilling* to take responsibility? Why? These reasons, excuses and considerations are limitations that prevent you from improving your game and creating your life the way you choose it to be.

**Accepting your role as creator is empowering.** You always have responsibility and you may choose a new point of view that supports the positive results you are truly willing to have on the golf course and in your life.

## CREATING PURPOSE AND DIRECTION

Purpose and direction are the context within which all your other results must agree. This is the direction you are moving. This is the value you derive within the actual chosen result. Accepting your purpose and direction creates opportunity for:

**Choice:** An alternative beyond decision, which is intuitive and does not require understanding.
**Clarity:** A specific image of the result you choose.

The following intentions create your **fundamental purpose and direction** and are essential to the life process. It is beneficial to read them aloud.

1.  I trust and love my body, mind, spirit and environment.
2.  I am free and open to experience.
3.  I experience humor and pleasure through my infinite creativity.
4.  I do only what contributes to my consciousness and the consciousness of others.
5.  I do only what contributes to the aliveness of the world around me.

**RESULTS YOU HAVE MANIFESTED**

Take a moment to consider results you have manifested in your golf game that *you value* and are willing to continue manifesting. Write them down.

1. _______________________________________________
2. _______________________________________________
3. _______________________________________________

You cannot eliminate anything in the physical world. You can only transform what you have created into something else, something that you prefer.

TRANSFORMATION is the ability to have an experience absent of form and is the only reliable indicator of a consciously evolving human being. Take a moment to consider results you have manifested in your golf game that *you do not value* and are willing to transform. Write them down.

1. _______________________________________________
2. _______________________________________________
3. _______________________________________________

Consider results you have manifested that *you do not value* now and how they are transformed. Example: if you tend to berate yourself after unsuccessful shots, stop and **be aware of how this reinforces negative outcomes.** Write them down.

1. _______________________________________________
2. _______________________________________________
3. _______________________________________________

Now, cross out the results *you do not value*. In writing down the lists of results that you value and do not value, you have defined where you are in your game.

**Be aware of the pitfalls of making change for the sake of change.** The reason so many of us become stuck in the "vicious circle of change" is we live within belief systems, which we did not consciously create. As mentioned earlier, these belief systems often come from our most negative belief: **"I'm not good enough."** These are reactive responses to former conditions or experiences, which do not support the evolution of our consciousness and the ability to exercise free will.

The result of this negative conditioning is we often confuse change with growth. That's why someone may change their golf equipment frequently instead of transforming the way they experience their game. One becomes accustomed to the vicious circle of change and the associated frustrations. **True growth only comes when we transform the way we play and approach our game.** Transformation requires, simultaneously, to be willing to risk having a new experience and to be aware of that experience.

## RESULTS YOU CHOOSE TO CREATE

You have defined manifested results in your game you value and manifested results you do not value. You have familiarized yourself with the vicious circle of change and what is required for transformation. In creating your list of chosen results you set the direction of your future. When choosing your results, understand how your golf game mirrors your life. When you make these choices, you are exercising your willingness to create and thereby **focusing vast potential and creative energy**.

1.  Begin by asking yourself the question: "What am I willing to have?" In your golf game. In your life.

2.  Do not limit what you are willing to have based on what you think is possible. This requires practice because, **as children, we were often taught to censor our creativity and dreams** to what adults considered "realistic" outcomes.

3. Do not limit what you are willing to have based on how you will get it. Do not get hung up in the process. Focus on the result you choose.

4. Imagine the entire result. Be aware of all aspects of the result including the circumstance and the consequences associated with having it.

5. Ask yourself: "If I could have it, would I take it?" (Be certain)

6. If answered "yes," consciously choose the result you are willing to have.

7. If answered "no," create and choose a different result.

- Write down your list of ten chosen results.
- **Read your list aloud each day** and update as your results are created.

## RESULTS I CHOOSE TO MANIFEST:

1. _______________________________________________
   _______________________________________________

2. _______________________________________________
   _______________________________________________

3. _______________________________________________
   _______________________________________________

4. _______________________________________________
   _______________________________________________

5. _______________________________________________
   _______________________________________________

6. _______________________________________________

_______________________________________________

7. _______________________________________________

_______________________________________________

8. _______________________________________________

_______________________________________________

9. _______________________________________________

_______________________________________________

10. ______________________________________________

_______________________________________________

You may consider choosing your list of results a momentary leap into the unknown. Make the choices. After your moment of uncertainty, you will experience the energy and physical lightness of consciously choosing.

## CHOOSING YOUR MANIFESTING RESULT

From your list of Chosen Results, choose a Manifesting Result. What is important about the Manifesting Result is what it does, not what it is. Your Manifesting Result clears the reactive brain and therefore allows you to create all the results you consciously choose. The criteria for choosing your Manifesting Result:

1. **Be certain** you are willing to have this result.
2. Visualize your Manifesting Result in present time, **as if fully accomplished.**
3. The result is achievable, that is, possible within our current collective belief system as human beings.

4.  Include yourself in the visualization to engender experience.
5.  **This result is the result** and not just a process toward the result you are creating.

**Perhaps the result is as simple as the satisfaction you experience with completion of a full, balanced swing; or maintaining an even temper throughout your round; or the thought of you stepping off the eighteenth green, a champion. The choice is yours.**

**YOUR CHOSEN MANIFESTING RESULT IS:**

_______________________________________________

_______________________________________________

Communication with your unconscious mind is best when you include the visual, verbal, emotional and mental aspects of your Manifesting Result. Visualization is optimized when you **integrate a complete sensory experience** involving the sight, touch, sound, smell, taste and emotional aspects.

Ask yourself what success looks like, feel the subtle vibration of the club in your hands, hear the club head make a crisp, solid pass through the ball, hold the finish of your swing and watch your shot fly toward the pin.

Experience your results at this new heightened level of sensory awareness, but most importantly at the emotional level. **How do you feel watching your shot sail toward the pin?** What is your experience? Are you satisfied? Is this enough?

The act of visualization, or imagining, embodies a new importance when you realize this is not daydreaming, but the act of providing your unconscious reactive mind with clear messages. Now, describe three Manifesting Result experiences. Describe them completely with enough sensory detail to have clarity and engender experience.

**MANIFESTING RESULT EXPERIENCES:**

Experience #1

Experience #2

Experience #3

**ACHIEVING RESULTS THROUGH DIRECT EXPERIENCE**

The Natale Manifesting material is based on proven methods, which have been used successfully for many years. Your belief in the methods presented is not important. These methods have been used in many different forms and do not require your belief. What is essential is for you to **use them as if they are true.**

As children, we loved to play. **As children, we were absent of limiting beliefs and achieved growth through direct experience.** Belief occurred *after* we experienced value.

USE > EXPERIENCE > KNOWLEDGE = VALUE (BELIEF)

As adults, we forget to play. As adults, we limit our growth by requiring belief before we are willing to experience. It is this **memory of experience**, which keeps us stuck in old beliefs and going round in the vicious circle of change. This memory of experience does not create new value and expanding consciousness.

(BELIEF) USE > MEMORY OF EXPERIENCE >
SAME KNOWLEDGE = OLD VALUES

Belief is an illusion. Use of the Natale Manifesting methods presented here allows you to move through experience directly to expanded consciousness and realization of your chosen results. Believing is only necessary when direct experience is lacking. Belief is a method of avoidance, which we create when we have insufficient direct experience of an idea we are expected to accept.

**The way you think about things determines their power.** This is evident in every aspect of your life and especially on the golf course. Expand your consciousness and manifest the results you choose through direct experience. Be aware. Do it now.

1.  Use your Manifesting Result at will. Notice how it feels to experience your golf game with this new level of sensory awareness.

2.  Review your chosen results daily and update as you will.

3.  Review your fundamental direction and purpose.

And, above all, don't take any of this too seriously. **There is no value in seriousness.** Have fun. Go play the game of your life.

Choose your targets wisely.
Consider where your next shot is best
played. Without choosing a specific
target and trajectory you will
most likely default to a variety
of other, less desired possibilities.

# LESSON 4: THE POWER OF YOUR BREATH

Breath is life. Every breath is a moment of growth followed by a moment of surrender. Your breath is the source of every golf swing, every laugh, every sigh. Awareness of the patterns of your breath is the gateway to controlling your energy and state of mind. A relaxed and heightened self-awareness creates emotional balance and is the key to exercising your free will on the golf course.

In our culture of expediency everything appears urgent. The competition for your attention is intense and relentless. In this pressurized environment, the mind easily wanders. For most people, breathing is rarely a thoughtful endeavor. Breathing is often shallow and incomplete. Vigorous use of the lungs is usually relegated to challenging aerobic exercise. Be aware of this.

Thousands of years ago, early yogis realized learning to breathe fully and evenly nurtured both the body and the mind. Modern physics theorizes matter and energy as similar manifestations only with varied density. Consider your body and mind in this way. "Prana" is what yogis call life energy. The practice of Pranayama is the control of energy and was developed to bring body and mind into balance through awareness of the breath. Pranayama is done by itself, and throughout your yoga practice, to promote clarity of mind and growth through a deeper understanding of the mind-body connection.

**EXERCISE**

- Lie on your back with your knees up.

- Employ the entire lungs. Fill your lower lungs, down into the belly. Fill your middle lungs, feel your ribs expand. Fill your upper lungs, high into your chest.

- Breathe in. Make it slow and easy.

- Breathe out. Feel your navel move gently toward your spine.

- As you inhale, direct your awareness and your breath to the greatest sensation you are feeling. Exhale and release the sensation. Repeat.

- Be aware of the rhythm of directing your awareness and releasing. Be relaxed. Be aware. It is easy to want to lose consciousness, to want to fall asleep, but stay with it.

BREATH IN – Experience growth and renewal, channel healing energy throughout every cell in your body.

BREATH OUT – Release, let go, surrender.

We repeat this pattern every moment of our lives. When we practice and when we play. This is the wellspring of your energy. Let your breath be the gateway to your self, to being certain, to releasing negative feelings and behavior. Notice if your breath pattern changes whenever you feel excited or challenged, when you are late for an appointment or about to discuss a contentious issue with a co-worker or loved one.

Notice shifts in your energy. Notice when your reactive mind injects some illusion of negative conditioning. You may always return to your breath. You may always change your pattern. Take a deep, full breath. Take in whatever you need. Whatever you want. Whenever you feel the need. Take a complete breath. Relax.

BREATH IN – Channel energy toward your chosen objective.

BREATH OUT – Let go and silence all other thoughts.

Whenever we feel anger, we are
not in the moment. What happens in the
now of present time is void of frustration,
struggle and the loss of self-control.
Get out of your head and into the moment.
Enjoy yourself.

# LESSON 5: STANDING POSTURES

People are often under the misconception yoga is a religion or a meditation technique. Yoga is a five-thousand-year-old science of life, which includes meditation as one component of a complete practice. Yogis are aware of the mind-body connection and the importance of proper exercise, diet and rest.

Meditation occurs spontaneously during yoga practice. Yoga meditation is the result of being present in posture, being aware of the deep and full rhythm of your breath and holding your focus effortlessly. Yoga meditation is the opposite of concentration, which is strenuous. Yoga meditation rises from holding the postures through several breath cycles, which dissolves stress and brings clarity and a sense of well being. With practice, these moments of clarity extend beyond the time you spend in postures and into your daily life. With practice, health and fitness are inevitable.

The primary purpose of the standing yoga postures presented here is to energize your body and promote strength, flexibility and range of motion. These are essential daily exercises for golf conditioning. The "Short Set" sequence should be done prior to practice sessions, before a round and during the round to keep your muscles stand joints warm and ready. It is always best to warm the body prior to doing any stretching or exercise.

Combined with the breathing techniques presented in the preceding lesson, these yoga postures will help you maintain flexibility and the mental and emotional balance necessary to execute each shot.

**OBJECTIVE: STABLE LOWER BODY, FLEXIBLE UPPER BODY**

**Exercise restraint. You should always consult your physician before beginning any physical fitness program. Never force anything.** There is no competition here. Do what you can do comfortably and no more. Move toward your physical edge carefully. Never bounce. Breathe into the moment. There is no need to look good. This is an opportunity to simply be.

**EXERCISE**

- Stand and notice your balance. Shift weight to all four corners of your feet.

- Notice your connection with the earth. Draw energy up from the ground and through your spine without becoming stiff.

- Be aware of your breath. Relax. Breathe deeply and slowly.

- Inhale – Grow and expand. Exhale – let go, surrender control.

- Inhale – Direct the breath to your greatest sensation.

- Exhale – Release.

During all the following standing postures, contract your thigh muscles to gently raise the kneecaps. Avoid over stretching and hyperextension of the knees.

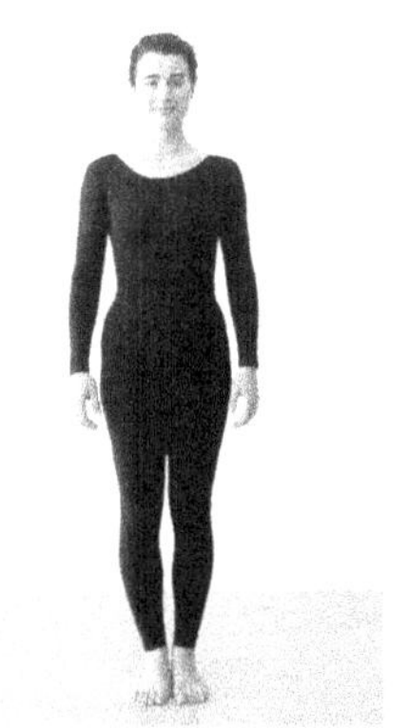  

**Balance** – The primary purpose of this posture is to steady yourself. Stand with your feet together, allowing your two legs to feel as one. Slowly shift your weight to the inside of your left foot. When you feel balanced, begin to raise your right foot. Take it as far up the left calf as you can without loosing balance. Take five full breaths. Lower the left foot slowly. Shift your weight to the inside of your right foot. When balanced, raise your left foot and repeat the process on this side with five full breaths.

**Neck Rolls** – Purpose here is to relax the muscles of the neck and upper back. Separate your feet to hip width. Begin with chin up. Initiate the rolls at the crown of the head. Let your head fall forward. Inhale, rotating slowly to the left and back. When you reach the top, exhale and let the head slowly rotate down and to the right. At the bottom, inhale and reverse the process, rotating slowly to the right and back. When you reach the top, exhale and let the head slowly rotate down and to the left. Repeat total of five cycles.

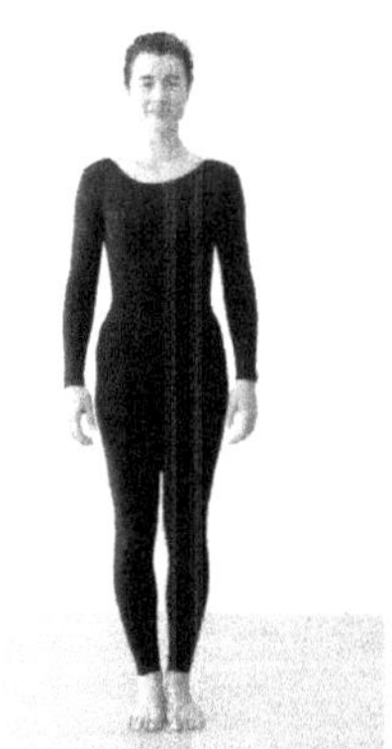  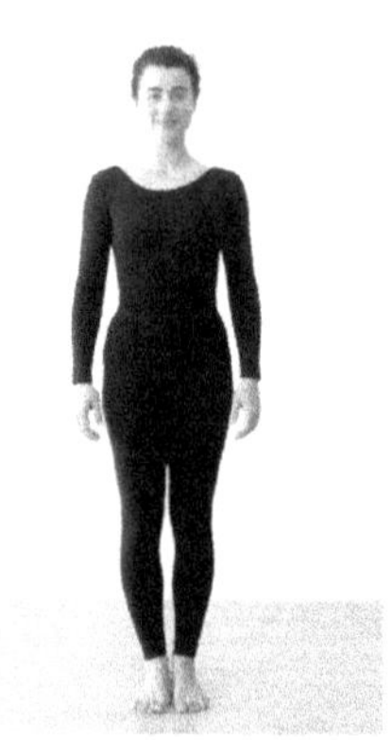

**Shoulder Lifts** – This posture is ideal for pre-shot stress relief. Roll your shoulders in a circular motion. Relax and let your shoulder blades slide down your back. Inhale, slowly raising your shoulders toward your ears. Exhale and allow the shoulder blades to slowly slide down your back. Repeat total of five cycles.

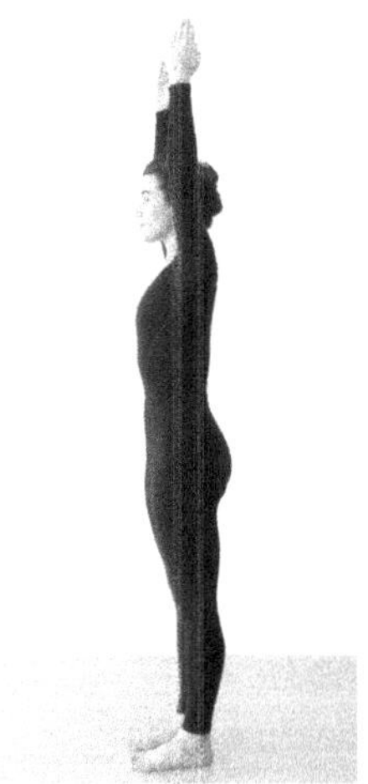  

**Half Sun Salute** – Inhale and raise your arms to the sky. Exhale, hinge from hips and allow your upper body to fall forward slowly. Don't force hands to ground. Take your hands to your shins. Straighten your arms and take a breath. Extend the top of your head away from your hips for a gentle spinal stretch. Exhale and allow the head to relax forward. Inhale, hinging at the hips, keep the belly lifted and raise upper body and arms back to start position. Repeat total of five times.

**Triangle** – Spread your legs 3-1/2 to 4 feet apart. Turn the left foot in 15 degrees and the right foot out 90 degrees. Inhale and raise your arms parallel to the ground. Exhale, shift the right hip into the left, slowly lower your right hand to your right leg, while keeping the body in one plane. *Go only as far as you can go comfortably.* With each exhale, gently move your left shoulder behind you. Take five complete breaths here. Inhale, slowly rise, return arms parallel to the ground. Turn the right foot in 15 degrees and the left foot out 90 degrees. Exhale, slowly lower your left hand to your left knee or thigh. With each exhale, gently move your right shoulder behind you. Take five complete breaths. Inhale, slowly return to start position.

**Triangle Extension** – Lengthen your stretch. Turn your left foot in 15 degrees and the right foot out 90 degrees. Inhale and raise your arms parallel to the ground. Exhale, shift the right hip into the left, slowly lower your right hand to your right knee or thigh and extend your left arm over your head. With each exhale, gently move your left shoulder behind you. Take five complete breaths.

Inhale, slowly rise, return arms parallel to the ground. Turn your right foot in 15 degrees and the left foot out 90 degrees. Exhale, shift the left hip into the right, slowly lower your left hand to your left knee or thigh and extend your right arm over your head. With each exhale, gently move your right shoulder behind you. Take five complete breaths. Inhale, slowly return to start position.

**Triangle Twist** – This posture enables increase in upper body range of motion and hips. Begin with your left foot forward, extend the right foot open. Inhale and raise your arms parallel to the ground. Exhale and turn your upper body until you are facing over your right foot. Inhale, rotate your upper body dropping your left hand to your leg and raising your right arm toward the sky. *Go as far as you can go comfortably.* Take five complete breaths.

Inhale and return to start position. Shift your right foot forward, extend the left foot open. Inhale and raise your arms parallel to the ground. Exhale and turn your upper body until you are facing over your left foot. Inhale, rotate your upper body dropping your right hand to your leg and raising your left arm toward the sky. Take five complete breaths. Inhale, slowly return to start position.

**Forward Bend** – Roll your shoulders. Exhale, hinge forward slowly at the hips and let your arms hang. Whatever you've been holding onto, let go of it now. Take five complete breaths here. Inhale and return to start position.

As part of your overall conditioning program, you may complete the eight-posture standing cycle, with the number of breaths indicated, in conjunction with the floor postures presented in the following lesson.

**THE SHORT SET ~**

**BEFORE PRACTICE OR PLAY OR DURING A ROUND**

For pre-practice or pre-round conditioning warm-ups, we recommend the following "Short Set" of standing postures and breath cycles. **Remember to go slowly and only as far as you can comfortably.**

**Neck Rolls** – Three cycles – inhale and allow your head to roll up and to the left. At the top, exhale and allow your head to roll back down to the right. Reverse direction. Inhale, roll to right. At the top exhale, back down to the left.

**Shoulder Lifts** – Five cycles – roll your shoulders in a circular motion. Relax and allow your shoulder blades to slide down your back. Inhale and raise shoulders toward ears. Exhale and allow shoulder blades to slide down your back. Repeat five cycles.

**Half Sun Salute** – Five cycles – inhale and raise your arms to the sky. Exhale and hinge at the hips. Take your hands down to knees or shins. Inhale and extend your head outward for a gentle spinal stretch. Exhale and allow your head to drop forward. Inhale, raise arms and hinge upper body back to start position. Repeat five cycles.

**Triangle Extension** – Two to three cycles – spread your legs 3-1/2 to 4 feet apart. Turn right foot in 15 degrees and left foot out 90 degrees. Inhale and raise your arms parallel to the ground. Exhale, shift the left hip into the right, lower your left hand to your left leg, while keeping the body in one plane. *Go only as far as you can comfortably*. With each exhale, gently move your right shoulder behind you. Take five complete breaths here. Next, extend your right arm and take five complete breaths. Return to start position and do the opposite side.

**Triangle Twist** – Two to three cycles – begin with your left foot forward. Inhale and raise your arms parallel to the ground. Exhale and turn your upper body until you are facing over your left foot. Inhale, rotate your upper body dropping the right hand to left thigh, raising your left arm toward the sky. *Go as far as you can go comfortably.* Take five complete breaths. Return to start position and do the opposite side.

Use any of these Short Set postures, and breath patterns, to stay warm and ready during practice or play. Take a moment, the next time you are on the practice tee, to notice how few people stretch before a practice session. If your golf companions give you any grief about what you are doing, notice their energy level, how much they are holding on. Then let it go. Avoid wasting your energy. Let your results speak for themselves. Your detractors will come around.

Do you finish your swing?
Club head control is destroyed
by deceleration. Keep your swing
in rhythm and accelerating.
Turn away. Turn through.

# LESSON 6: FLOOR POSTURES

The primary purpose of the yoga floor postures presented here is to cool the body while promoting strength, flexibility and range of motion. The floor postures are an integral component of your regular stretching routine, which you may do at home in the mornings and/or evenings after you complete the standing postures presented in the previous lesson.

*Again, exercise restraint.* Never force or strain anything. Do what you can do comfortably and no more. Move toward your physical edge carefully. Never bounce. Breathe into the moment. Stretch. Reach for something you want.

- Be aware of your breath. Relax. Breathe deeply and slowly.
- Inhale – grow and expand. Exhale – let go, surrender control.
- Inhale – direct the breath to your greatest sensation.
- Exhale – release.

**Table Pose** – This gentle spinal stretch begins with your knees hip width apart and your hands shoulder width apart with your spine and neck in a straight and neutral position. Inhale, slowly raise your head toward the ceiling while lowering your torso toward the floor. Like a cat, exhale and slowly lower your head while arching your back toward the ceiling without squeezing the shoulders to the ears. Repeat this cycle a total of five times.

**Child's Pose** – An excellent resting posture, this spinal stretch begins from the neutral Table Pose. Exhale and allow your hips to fall back toward your heels while lowering your forehead to the floor. *Only go as far as you can go comfortably*. Extend your hands and arms in front of you. Take five complete breaths (or as many more as you like). Let go.

**Pigeon Pose** – This is a deep gluteus and hip opener. *Go slowly and only as far as you feel comfortable.* From the neutral Table Pose, cross your left knee over your right. Stretch your right leg back, bringing the thigh parallel to the floor. Keep your hips square, lower your torso toward the floor. Keep the bent knee slightly outside the hip. *Go as far as you can comfortably.* Take five complete breaths.

Roll to your left side and straighten the left leg. Rest for a moment or two. Return to neutral position and do the opposite side. From the neutral Table Pose cross your right knee over your left. Stretch your left leg back, bringing the thigh parallel to the floor. Keep your hips square, lower your torso toward the floor. Keep the bent knee slightly outside the hip. *Go as far as you can comfortably.* Take five complete breaths.

Roll to your right side and straighten the right leg. Rest a moment or two. Return to neutral position. Lower your hips to your heels. Rest in Child's Pose and breathe.

**Half Spinal Twist** – Lie on your back with legs extended. Raise your right knee and place your right foot flat on the floor. Place your left hand on your right knee. Inhale. Exhale and allow your right knee to cross over the left side of your body toward the floor. Keep both shoulders on the floor. Move slowly. *Go only as far as you can go comfortably*. Extend your right arm and turn your head to the right. Take five complete breaths here.

Release your right knee and return to start position. Extend your right leg. Raise your left knee and place your left foot flat on the floor. Place your right hand on your left knee. Inhale. Exhale and allow your left knee to cross over the right side of your body toward the floor. Keep both shoulders on the floor. Move slowly. *Go only as far as you can go comfortably*. Extend your left arm and turn your head to the left. Take five complete breaths. Release your left knee and return to start position.

**Seated Twist** – Sit on the floor comfortably with your legs extended. Raise your left knee and cross your left foot over your right leg until flat on the floor. Exhale, extend your left arm above and behind you. Turn your left shoulder and place your left hand on the floor behind you. Extend your right arm then place your right elbow outside your left knee. Inhale and lift the spine. Exhale and twist away from the knee. Allow the head to follow for a deeper twist. Take five complete breaths here.

Raise your right arm and rotate your shoulders. Return to start position. Extend your left leg and shake it out. Raise your right knee and cross your right foot over your left leg until flat on the floor. Exhale, extend your right arm above and behind you. Turn your right shoulder and place your right hand on the floor behind you. Extend your left arm then place your left elbow outside your right knee. Inhale and lift the spine. Exhale and twist away from the knee. Allow the head to follow for a deeper twist. Take five complete breaths here.

Raise your right arm and rotate your shoulders. Return to start position. Extend your left leg and shake it out.

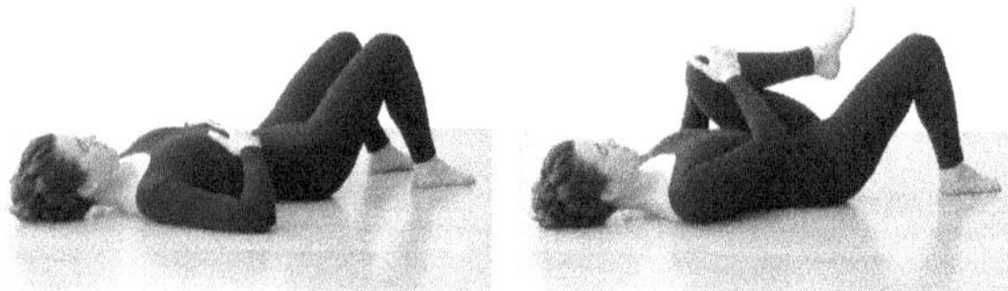

**Lower Back Releases, single** – Strengthen the abdominal muscles with these moderate stretches. Turn over on your back with knees bent. As you exhale allow your navel to drop toward your spine. Tilt your pelvis so your hips and the small of your back are flat against the floor. Inhale and lift your left leg to your chest. Exhale and lower your left foot to the floor. Repeat this a dozen times. More as you feel comfortable. Repeat the same number with your right leg. When complete, pull your knees to your chest. Rock gently from side to side.

**Lower Back Releases, double** – More abdominal conditioning. On you back with knees bent, exhale and allow your navel to drop toward your spine. Tilt your pelvis so your hips and the small of you back are flat against the floor. Inhale and lift both legs to your chest. Exhale and lower your feet to the floor. Repeat this a dozen times. More as you feel comfortable. When complete, pull your knees to your chest. Rock gently from side to side.

**Forward Bend** – From the seated position, sit comfortably and shake out your legs. *Go only as far as you can comfortably*. Extending your arms, hinge at the hips and allow your torso to stretch up and out of the lower back then fall forward toward your legs. Breathe deeply. Let go. Take five complete breaths. When complete, lie down and pull both your knees into your chest and rock side to side to release the lower back.

**Relaxation** – Complete the postures by lying flat on the ground. Close your eyes. Let your arms and legs go. Let your shoulders and hips go. Feel your body relax. Inhale breathing deep into your lungs: fill belly, ribs and chest. Exhale releasing: belly, ribs and chest. Allow yourself to relax. Notice how this feels.

**Schedule time to practice these postures**. If you complete the standing and floor series at least three times a week you will experience greater flexibility and range of motion almost immediately. It is especially important to do the recommended "Short Set" series of standing postures before you practice, before you play and as you feel the need during your round.

These postures are not intended to replace your current exercise program. Depending on your age and physical condition, we suggest moderate strength and cardiovascular training sessions at least three times each week. **Consult with your physician before beginning any exercise program**. Once they say it's okay, go for it. Begin slowly and stick with it.

You are also encouraged to consider taking regular yoga classes at a yoga studio or health club in your community.

Exercise imagination. Before every shot, recall the purest shot you've ever played. When you complete your swing practice holding a balanced finish until the ball hits the ground.

# LESSON 7: SHOT VISUALIZATION

s children we lived and played in an imaginary world where anything was possible. Soon enough our innocent, playful behavior fell from favor. We were encouraged – gently or harshly – to "grow up" and "stop acting childish" by the adults and older children around us. Criticism and admonitions such as "stop daydreaming" and "who do you think you are?" began to distort our view of the world. Most of us accept this adult belief system and stop exercising the power of our imagination.

Much has been written about visualization. Earlier in The Choice to Think lesson we presented the importance of going beyond your belief systems to having **direct experience**. This way you are confident who you are and what you will accomplish. Shot visualization is a simple yet powerful technique that **sets your mind and body into alignment**. This process "locks in" your target because, in your mind, you have already experienced complete success.

You are encouraged to **incorporate visualization into the seamless efficiency of a consistent pre-shot routine**. Rather than drilling a succession of balls on the practice tee, consider going through each shot practicing your pre-shot routine. Notice the difference in the quality of your practice with this approach. Notice the difference when your practice mirrors actual on-course situations.

**EXERCISE**

1. Know your distance. Consider the situation and the shot you will play. Choose your club.

2. Standing behind the ball, select your target line and take a deep breath. Inhale and exhale and recall the purest shot you've ever played. Notice how the club feels in your hands. Roll your shoulders. Make a confident practice swing.

3. Set your clubface behind the ball. Step into the shot. Your alignment and posture are square. Take one last look at your target.

4. Your tempo is excellent. Back and through. You strike the ball perfectly with a full extension. Balanced at finish, you hold this position until the ball lands.

Take your pre-shot visualization onto the putting green. Get low to the ground. Study the slope and direction of the grain. Know your distance. Align your putt. In your mind, recall a clutch putt you've made recently and see this ball rolling into the cup. Take a breath. Inhale. Exhale. Make a confident practice stroke. Address the ball. Back and through. Head still. Only look up in time to watch the putt drop.

You have been visualizing at some level already. The key is to have a complete sensory experience of success *before every shot*. It only takes a second to do this as part of your pre-shot routine. Practice consistently and watch what happens.

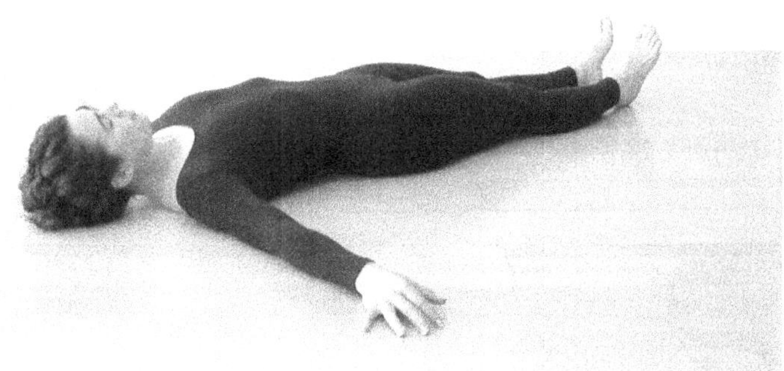

## EXERCISE

Find your way to the ground. Lie on your back with knees up if that is more comfortable. Focus on your breath. Relax. Inhale – growth. Exhale – surrender. Inhale. Exhale. Take a moment here for yourself.

1. Think of all the positive things you've accomplished in your life.
2. Think of all the people who love and respect you.
3. Recall a glorious moment in your life, on or off the golf course.
4. Remember how confident you felt in that moment.
5. How the air smelled. The color of the sky. The sounds around you.
6. Know you created this moment. It is your experience. Uniquely yours.
7. Claim this moment as your own. Be confident.
8. Know you can do this at will. Because you can.

As a player, you understand every day and every round provides a fresh start, a new beginning. If you step onto the first tee with an open mind and a confident attitude you are well on your way. If you exercise your imagination on every shot, then anything is truly possible. Imagine that.

As you practice, develop swing keys
to minimize your thought processes.
Focus on the feeling of satisfaction realized
from making a complete, fluid swing.

# LESSON 8: STRATEGIC CONSIDERATIONS

Most of the following golf tips are common knowledge. We present them here as a reminder so you may incorporate them as you practice. This way, during a round, you don't have to stop and think. Unnecessary thought processes stall the flow of your game and your pace of play.

Incorporating these strategic considerations frees your mind and builds confidence. Allow your heightened sense of effectiveness to manifest itself in a quiet and gracious manner. Conserve your energy. Be clear about your intentions and your ability to manifest them.

1. **Choose your result, your target** – Consider the optimum place from which to play your next shot and make a choice. Play for position.

2. **Hold the thought of the best swing you've ever made** – Regardless of the club selection, your body knows exactly what to do. Be confident. Be balanced.

3. **Visualize every shot** – Have a complete sensory experience, the feel and flight and roll, then allow each shot to happen. See every putt going into the cup.

4. **Swing within yourself** – Aggressive or quick swings are symptomatic of emotional imbalance and rarely achieve the intended result.

5. **Get the ball to the hole** – Know your distance and use enough club. This choice allows a confident swing without overpowering the ball.

6. **Play one shot at a time** – Allow yourself to be in the moment. Let go of errant shots immediately. Be confident you will recover.

7. **Be ready to play** – Evaluate your next shot when you approach the ball. Consider the distance, the wind, topography, stance and target.

8. **Avoid watching other players swing** – Unless their action is exceptional, stand aside and catch the flight of their ball. Avoid the influence of other's flaws.

9. **Fundamentals** – Remain mindful of proper grip, posture, alignment and tempo. Be aware of ball positioning. Keep your head still.

10. **Breathe and stretch** – Stay warm and ready both physically and emotionally. This is particularly important before critical shots and late in the round.

11. **You are what you eat** – Fuel your body with sufficient water and nutrition throughout the round. Avoid sugar, caffeine and alcohol.

12. **Practice your short game** – At least half your practice should be wedges, chipping and putting. Practice everything but focus on scoring.

Be positive and supportive of yourself and others. Consider the possibility, even in your regular weekend game, of avoiding unnecessary chatter on the course. This would include the discussion of politics, family problems, root canals or anything that creates tension among your playing companions. Think about what puts you at ease and what stresses you out. If someone attempts to needle you a little, that's something else. Have fun. Deal with them as you will but avoid participation in chatter that creates distraction and drains your energy. Play golf.

Most importantly, laugh at yourself. **Golf is a game to be played and enjoyed. Don't be too serious about anything, especially golf.** If you're serious you will create tension and inevitably find yourself over griping, swinging out of your shoes and spraying shots. Employ a strategy to maintain your balance and exercise your imagination. Play from that place and keep it on the short grass.

Be aware of your grip pressure.
If it tends to be too tight, consider
what is happening. Relax the tension
so you may release the club.

# LESSON 9: FOCUS ON YOUR FINISH

We have explored making the choice to think and how to man-ifest chosen results. We have demonstrated the power of your breath, how to relax and channel your energy. The yoga pos-tures focus your attention and enhance your flexibility and range of mo-tion. Pre-shot visualization, proper instruction and practice build confi-dence and create a fluid, consistent swing.

Here we address the two most common flaws in developing golf swings: the lack of even tempo and the loss of balance.

## EXERCISING TEMPO AND BALANCE

Take an iron in your hands. Place your feet together and balance yourself. Shift your weight to the inside of your feet and balance on the balls of your feet. Keeping your head still, slowly rotate your shoulders, moving the club head back and through in a foot-long path. Feel a subtle weight shift from forward to back. Forward to back. Repeat this motion several times then extend the club head path to eighteen inches. Repeat this motion, back and through, back and through, until you establish a comfortable tempo. Keep extending the club head path until you reach a half swing. Back and through. Back and through.

Widen your stance to shoulder width. Choose your target. Address the ball and set your grip, stance and alignment. Think about the flight of the shot you've chosen and feel the satisfaction of solid contact as the club head passes through the ball. Consider your swing as *three fluid seamless* components:

ADDRESS – Square your stance and alignment.

BACK SWING – Turn away from the target until you reach the top.

THROUGH SWING – Turn your hips toward the target until hips and chest are square to the target line. Hold your balance here.

BACK SWING > THROUGH SWING > BALANCED FINISH

**Focus on your finish. Focus on your result.** Completing your swing with an even tempo and a balanced finish are the keys to consistent shot making. Tempo and balance enable you to keep the club head on plane and bring it square through impact. Mastering tempo and balance create confidence and generates power. There is no need to make an aggressive swing. A harder swing may accelerate club head speed, but it also destroys your tempo, moves the club head off plane and throws you off balance. If you've been playing golf for any length of time you probably have learned this lesson more than once.

## SWING THOUGHT (MANTRA)

You may find it helpful, when you are on the golf course, to have a simple word or mantra that aligns your mind-body considerations. You don't want to ponder the mysteries of the universe as you address every shot. Choose a word that embodies the mind-body connection you've practiced. Choose a word that sets you at ease and makes you feel confident.

Two-syllable words, as demonstrated in the following exercises, are ideal. You may repeat your mantra to yourself during the round and use as your primary swing thought. Consider a word that expresses how you want your golf swing to be and give it a try. Address the ball. Raise and drop your shoulders. Relax. Repeat the word. Now, incorporate your breath into your complete swing.

BREATHE – Inhale smooth and easy, extend your exhale.

INHALE – Turn your back away from the target.

EXHALE – Turn your hips toward target. Finish balanced and square to target.

**EXERCISE**

As an experiment, practice repeating the mantra during your swing. The first syllable is for your back swing. The second syllable is for your through swing. This may seem awkward the first couple of passes, but practice until you feel comfortable, until it seems automatic. As example, use the swing thought "WILL-FULL" and remember to breathe.

"WILL" > BACK SWING – Inhale, turn away from the target.

"FULL" > THROUGH SWING – Exhale, turn your hips toward the target.

BALANCED FINISH – Complete with hips and chest facing the target.

Find a word that brings everything into alignment (i.e. ease-y, grace-ful, re-lax, com-plete, pow-er). Practice your swing thought consistently. This exercise is great for establishing tempo. Play around until you feel comfortable.

In conclusion, commit to working with an instructor to develop reliable fundamentals. Recognize the importance of physical conditioning. Increase your flexibility and range of motion. Breathe and relax. Let go of any behavior or belief that does not support the results you choose.

There is nothing gained by holding on. Loosen up. Enjoy your game completely. See every shot clearly and let it happen. Allow yourself the satisfaction of playing golf in a heightened state of awareness certain you choose what is possible.

Play well.

When you feel pressure or stress,
take three complete breaths.
Inhale and take what you need.
Exhale and let it go.
Silence all other thoughts.

# EPILOGUE

I changed my mind about golf in a moment. On an unusually gray California winter day many years ago, I found my drive 70 yards from the green in a tight lie. This was a relatively simple second shot to a short par four, which I'd played dozens of times. But I caught the shot thin and bladed the ball over the green. In a moment, watching in disbelief, I experienced frustration and anger for blowing such an easy scoring opportunity. And then I laughed.

Instead of cursing the situation and tossing my club, I laughed and set about saving par. I looked up at the dull sky and the swaying palms and promised to maintain my composure, visualize each shot and complete the round with my integrity intact. There were other challenges that day, but my patience and focus were rewarded with a string of three birdies on the back nine. The round was a turning point. Not for the score I posted, but for the way I was able to maintain my mental and emotional composure.

I was encouraged and incorporated more yoga postures and breathwork into my game. There was immediate improvement and I began to share my experiences. The process of creating the Will of Golf program required two years and included application of manifesting techniques learned from my mentor Frank Natale. My yoga teacher Leeann Carey helped refine the yoga posture sequences. A series of early Will of Golf workshops in her Hermosa Beach studio confirmed the benefits of improved balance and flexibility. Learning how to relax while maintaining focus struck a major chord with all participants.

We trust the Will of Golf program will serve you. Give it time. Be clear about your intentions and the results you choose. Find an instructor and develop your game. Practice and play with purpose and intent. Above all, lighten up and enjoy the rewards of being in the moment. We're confident you will discover new levels of satisfaction in your game and improve your performance.

Ralph

The concept of "grip it and rip it"
creates tension and breaks your
natural rhythm. Instead, think
"load and unload" as you move
through the ball to a complete
and balanced finish.

# APPENDIX

The following articles by Ralph Cissne were featured in 2002 issues of *Southern California Golf.*

THE MIND-BODY CONNECTION:

## THE GREATEST PUTTER WHO EVER LIVED

Every golfer experiences moments of doubt. No other game provides more opportunities for gut checks and self-evaluation. Who hasn't been humbled in the following manner? With great skill, you hit an excellent approach shot, bow gracefully to the thunderous applause of your companions and walk triumphantly onto the green. Then you stand over a four-foot birdie putt and feel the cold and certain clutch of fear grip your throat? "What if I miss it?" you ask yourself, initiating the probability of failure. "I will look like a fool." A better question is, "What are you thinking?"

Whether it is a four-foot birdie putt or a 190-yard carry over water, fear is the beginning of the end of your scoring opportunity. Fear in these situations often rises from reflex reactions to our most negative fundamental thought about ourselves, which for many people is: "I am not good enough." As a child your family, friends or teachers may have used harsh words to criticize you or your behavior. They may have said you couldn't do this or that. It is not unusual for a small child to accept such statements as fact. They are not. Such criticism is often intended to protect us; however, these misguided negative offerings can cut deep. Find a way to forgive these detractors, let go of the past and move on. What's the purpose of holding on to thoughts that bring you down? Better to choose a point of view that serves your objectives now. The world is how you perceive it to be. Ultimately, it is our responsibility to make the most of the opportunities we've created, in life and on the golf course.

"Everyone misses four-foot putts," you hear people say, but there is no logical reason to think about missing them. Golfers frequently make statements like, "I can't hit a three iron." or "I can't putt on these greens." How can promoting incompetence possibly help them improve their scores? The intelligent choice is to focus on the result. On the greens, take a few deep breaths, visualize the ball rolling along your chosen line and dropping into the center of the cup. See this clearly in your mind. Tell yourself you are **the greatest putter who ever lived.** Share this affirmation with your regular foursome. Amuse yourself, have some fun, knowing when you relax and fill your mind with positive imagery and a sense of accomplishment, there is no room for fear and failure.

Learn to build momentum in your round by feeding off your great shots. When you hit an iron close to the pin, rather than jumping up and down and screaming gratuities to the golf gods, choose to maintain your emotional balance. Smile and politely tip your cap to your companions, but conserve and redirect your energy. Relax and be aware of the profound sense of satisfaction flowing through your body. Be confident and know you may access this heightened state of accomplishment whenever you want. Relax, enjoy the moment and focus your attention on making the putt because you are, after all, "the greatest putter who ever lived."

There is no substitute for good instruction and plenty of practice. Practice with purpose and confidence. Develop a consistent pre-shot routine to align your body and lock in your intended target. If you really want to improve, commit to a teacher and a regular practice schedule with heavy emphasis on wedges, chipping and putting. The more confidence you build into your short game, the more success you will experience overall. And don't be seduced by the dreaded demons of distance. What's the point of being long and wrong? Learn to hit it straight first then go for distance.

Most importantly, focus on the finish, on what you truly want to accomplish. Practice visualizing the flight of your shots and, when you complete your swing, hold a balanced finish until our ball lands on the target. Maintaining balance is essential to building a consistent, fluid tempo. Lighten up and loosen your grip on your old bad habits. Think of your swing as an expression of your natural rhythm. Hold that thought and learn to take deep breaths to release the tension in your body. Learn to relax and embrace the possibilities of playing the game of your life. Celebrate your great shots and don't beat yourself up should something go wrong. Be confident you will recover. The beauty of golf is there is always room for redemption. Remember, you are the greatest… Play well.



# ENGAGING YOUR GOLF POWERHOUSE

Power has been a raging hot topic in golf for most of my life. We're all mad with the desire for greater distance, especially off the tee. Everyone wants to generate more power, but our new high-tech alloy equipment only provides the means to transfer energy as the club head strikes the ball. Ultimately, power is something you must find and cultivate within yourself.

I'm a bit of a purist about the game and was slow to surrender my sweet persimmon driver. It's a beautiful club and has held a special place in my closet for a very long time now. I'm not going to give up thirty yards off the tee. Who would? But once we have all the technology we can handle, then what? If you truly want to improve your game, lessons are always on the agenda. Work with your local golf professional to develop strong fundamentals of grip, stance and alignment. Balance, fluid tempo and bringing the club head down the line with consistency are the keys to success. Learning, and practicing, proper swing mechanics are mandatory if you want to increase your skills and self-confidence. This is also the gateway to your power.

## GET LEANER, LONGER AND STRONGER

Physical conditioning is also important. Go to any driving range and notice the people who stretch before they practice. Most people just drop the bucket and start swinging away. True athletes wouldn't think of practicing or playing without warming up and stretching the muscle groups involved. Virtually every professional athlete works with strength and conditioning coaches and trainers to optimize performance. This is particularly important if they have injuries. Why should golf be any different? Your local health club most likely has a certified personal trainer who can help you create proper stretches and "core conditioning" exercises based on your level of fitness.

Given the enormous popularity, you probably have a Hatha Yoga studio nearby. Yoga classes are an excellent way to increase your balance, strength, flexibility and range of motion. The stretches you learn from a trainer are almost certainly based on aspects of this five-thousand-year-old science of life. Modern physics theorizes matter and energy are similar manifestations only with varied density. Consider your body and mind in this way. In yoga postures the breath is used to direct attention to the point of the greatest sensation. This process of concentrating energy promotes growth and healing of the muscles and connective tissues. The beauty of yoga, taught by experienced and inspired teachers, is the classes are self-contained. You find everything you need to get leaner, longer and stronger in one place.

## THE POWERHOUSE OF CONDITIONING

The purpose of Hatha Yoga is to fuse the body into an instrument of the will, which makes an ideal discipline for golfers. I discovered golf and yoga in my early teens. In my twenties I sustained lower back injuries and quickly learned, if I wanted to continue playing golf, I had to maintain my core strength and flexibility. So, over twenty years later, I practice yoga every morning and hit the golf ball longer than ever. Of course, I'm not using my old persimmon driver anymore.

The Pilates Method is another mind-body discipline, which blends the best of Western and Eastern approaches into exercises performed on mats or special equipment. Pilates exercises condition the entire body with special emphasis on the specific core muscle groups supporting the spine and pelvis. Called the Powerhouse, this group of muscles includes the rectus abdominis, internal obliques, lower back muscles, transversus abdominis and gluteus maximus. To engage your Powerhouse, pull your navel in toward your spine. Try this, lengthening from the center of your body when you stretch, walk or swing. As a golfer, you should immediately recognize the benefits of conditioning these muscles to help prevent injuries and promote a fluid and powerful golf swing.

## RELAX AND BE IN THE MOMENT

Extraordinarily hard swings destroy your accuracy and the rhythm of your round. How can you maintain balance and tempo when you are swinging out of your shoes? Yoga teachers encourage students to "find your center," the place in your body where you are balanced and complete. In yoga you learn how to breathe and that every breath is a moment of growth followed by a moment of surrender. A heightened state of relaxed self-awareness is a natural result of this process. With yoga practice, your physical and emotional balance is maintained, and you enjoy a meditative quality, which is easily accessed on the golf course and throughout your daily life. All that is required is to take a deep, full breath. Take in whatever is necessary. Then relax and enjoy the power of being in the moment.

## THE MIND-BODY CONNECTION:

## GOLFERS WEAR SOME FUNNY SHOES

My golf shoes were falling apart. One day, I looked down and they were coming unglued. I loved those shoes and hadn't noticed the wear. I worked in golf pro shops through high school and college and have always been particular about my equipment, especially the shoes. I wore tour-line white buck street shoes and cordovan tassel loafers in high school without the slightest hassle. Golf in Oklahoma, where I grew up, was held in the highest regard. And everyone knew golfers wear some funny shoes.

I'm driving to the golf store listening to the final minutes of a Lakers' playoff game and it gets intense. Kobe Bryant pulls his fourth quarter magic. I sit in my car spellbound. The Lakers win in the final seconds. It was quite a finish. I stroll up to the door of the golf store. It's locked. "Sorry," the attendant smiled through the glass. "We close at 5:00 on Sunday." So, I play another round in rotting shoes. No one noticed the condition of my old shoes, but when I finally had new ones (I bought two pair on sale), everyone gave me the business. I wouldn't call this pressure; it is just the natural gas that goes along with playing golf. Like some guy wearing a goofy polo shirt covered with smiling golf balls has a license to criticize anyone.

## LOOKING GOOD WHEN THE HEAT IS ON

Beyond looking good, how do you learn to hold up, even prosper, under the pressure of competition? Ultimately, this is what the mind-body connection is all about. "If I'm so good," you may ask, "Then why are my palms sweating and my heart beating so fast?" When I was in college, my partner and I were all square with three holes to play in a four-ball match. Our motivation to win was enhanced, as our opponents this day were particularly obnoxious. I had a thirty-foot putt for birdie on the sixteenth green, slightly down-hill and drifting right close to the hole. My partner gave me his read and stepped aside. I held my old Bullseye putter up to plumb the line and started backing up. One step. Two steps. Three steps. Then I found myself falling backward into space. I hung there, suspended in mid-air, for what seemed like a moment or two. I surrendered to the inevitable and landed flat on my back in the green side bunker.

"What are you doing?" my partner said. "Get out of there." I laughed and was on the verge of hysterics as he extended his hand and helped me to my feet. I dusted the sand off my clothes and raked the trap. Our opponents were not amused by the delay. I missed the birdie putt, but they missed theirs as well. We lost the match 2 and 1. A stroke of luck for them, but all I could think about was the view when I was flat on my back in that bunker. Nothing but blue sky. I just couldn't take the situation seriously after that.

## LEARNING TO GET OUT OF YOUR OWN WAY

Jump forward to a few years ago. I have a short wedge shot to an easy par four. I caught the ball thin and air mailed it over the green. Rather than scream and curse the cruelty of the golf gods, I thought about the view from that green side bunker when I was on my back. Blue sky and dancing leaves. I laughed and went about saving my par. My playing companions complemented me on how well I maintained my composure. "It was the wise choice," I quipped. "Took quite a few years to figure that out."

In yoga practice we breathe and stretch and release tension. It's a natural rhythm, which conditions you to "go with the flow" and learn to relax simply by taking a deep, circular breath and staying in the moment. Perhaps life isn't as complicated as we often think. Bringing awareness to behavior patterns that serve you, and those that do not, helps you gain perspective and move in the direction you choose to go. Opening your mind and loosening your grip on your bad habits allows you to let go of negative thoughts quickly. And perhaps you will learn to laugh at the lessons brought your way.

In yoga practice you leave your shoes at the door. Our Will of Golf program provides a framework to increase your flexibility, range of motion and power. You learn how to breathe and relax, to visualize and create great shots. The book and group seminars are based on timeless yoga and manifesting techniques to help you "get out of your own way" on the golf course. Ultimately, this is the biggest lesson to learn. Golf has a unique way of maintaining our humility. The best we can do is keep life in perspective and have some fun along the way. And golf is certainly more fun when you are playing your best.

# ABOUT THE AUTHOR

A lifelong student of the game, Ralph Cissne provides a unique and entertaining perspective for improving your mind-body approach and golf performance.

Cissne began working with Frank Natale in 1986, and adapted aspects of the Natale course *Results: The Willingness to Create* for golf based on his personal experience with these techniques. Cissne practiced and studied with Planet Yoga founder Leeann Carey for many years. Will of Golf breathing exercises and yoga postures are drawn from the Planet Yoga Method promoting strength, flexibility, balance, and personal discovery.

A native Californian, Cissne grew up playing golf in Oklahoma and graduated from The University of Oklahoma School of Journalism. He returned to Los Angeles in 1987 and was a longtime member of the Southern California PLGA. As a creative strategist, Cissne has created category-leading marketing programs for many innovative health and fitness brands including StairMaster Sports/Medical Products.

In addition to *Will of Golf*, Cissne is the author of *Prudence in Hollywood and Other Stories*, *Angel City Singles*, and *Don't Be Shy*. He currently lives in Oklahoma where he writes, plays golf, and serves as a life skills mentor for middle school students.

For more information visit willofgolf.com or ralphcissne.com.

# ACKNOWLEDGEMENTS

I was blessed with amazing parents from The Greatest Generation who encouraged me to play and an aunt and uncle who challenged me to think. Golf was a natural choice as I considered the game a complete athletic and psychological experience.

Growing up in the suburbs of Oklahoma City I participated in the junior golf program. During high school I was fortunate to work at Lake Hefner Golf Club where I played a lot of golf during my formative years. At Lake Hefner I learned valuable lessons about golf and life from professionals Joe Walser Jr., Norman Fleshman, Jim Awtrey, and Alsie Hyden. I am grateful to Golf Inc. for my college scholarship support and acknowledge golf friends through the years especially Steve Teter, Joe Roberts, Pope Van Cleff, Jeff and Stormy Williams, Ed Hanson, and Bruce Anderson.

Frank Natale, my friend and mentor, passed shortly after the original *Will of Golf* book was published. Frank's encouragement and contribution included insights from his course *Results: The Willingness to Create* presented in "The Choice to Think" lesson.

And thanks to Leeann Carey, my long-time yoga teacher for her enlightened instruction and friendship. In addition to her student and teacher trainings, Leeann has shared her yoga with many professional athletes and sports teams including the Los Angeles Lakers.

# RESOURCES

The following books and resources are offered for your consideration.

**Five Lessons: The Modern Fundamentals of Golf**
by Ben Hogan

**Harvey Penick's Little Red Book**
by Harvey Penick

**Golf is Not a Game of Perfect**
by Dr. Bob Rotella

**Still the Mind**
by Alan Watts

**Tao Te Ching**
translated by Stephen Mitchell

**Restorative Yoga Therapy**
by Leeann Carey

**Yoga The Iyengar Way**
Silva, Mira & Shyam Mehta

**Results: The Willingness to Create**
by Frank Natale
franknatale.com

**The Rules of Golf**
USGA Members Program
usga.org

# EXPERIENCING OM

The original *Will of Golf* booklet included an "OM (bilateral alignment)" CD created by Frank Natale for his personal use. Om often played on a continuous loop in his living space. Three 20-minute tracks (Mega Om, Flying Om, and Mother Om) were dedicated to Swami Baba Mutktananda, Frank's spiritual teacher.

To a yogi, no sound, word or symbol is more powerful. As Frank described: "Om is an ancient Sanskrit word symbolizing the phenomenal energy vibrations of reality or creation; the primal sound from which the whole of creation was manifested; a synonymous term for God. Traditional use is to evoke the awareness of source.

"Om embraces all aspects of life and grants all its rewards. Practicing the Om nourishes the inner being. Imparts spiritual strength. Purifies the brain and the heart. Just as we adorn our physical bodies with clothes and exercise to maintain health, so must we take care of our soul, our inner spiritual body, so that it develops naturally towards the beauty of ecstatic living."

The following meditation and sacred music albums are ones I enjoy, all available on most digital music platforms. Consider listening to 528 Hz music, which has shown, in as little as 5 minutes, potential for reducing stress and promoting relaxation. What's important is to experience this state of mind, in conjunction with deep relaxed breathing, so you may summon the peace and clarity whenever needed.

**Om (bilateral alignment)**
Frank Natale

**The Lightness of Being**
Anugama

**Shamanic Dream**
Anugama

**Officium**
Jan Garbarek & The Hilliard Ensemble

**El-Hadra**
Klaus Weise, Ted de Jong

The following pages are provided so you may journal about your new golf approach. Writing down declarations and results sends signals to your unconscious mind that you are in charge and making things happen. Again, don't take it too seriously. Trust the process for improvement.

1.  **Declarations** – Begin with a list of declarations, not hopes and dreams, but clear statements **about your game as if they are true**. It's powerful to read these statements aloud every day or before you practice or play. Declare: I am the greatest putter who every lived. I complete every swing in balance. I am the most improved player in my club. My iron play is spectacular. My short game is flawless. I am the club champion. I am…

2.  **Results** – Record the results of your practice sessions, matches, and scores. Note date, location, fairways hit and greens in regulation, number of putts, birdies, milestones, how much you enjoyed the round.

3.  **Instruction** – Journal about swing thoughts and tips from your instructor, articles or videos. Expand beyond "positive thinking" to "positive being" as you lighten your grip and release the club.

Beyond statistics, notice shifts in your attitude, improved balance, and your ability to stay focused. You may also journal about how experiences in your life impact your play. Know your reality is created by your thoughts. And that you may always change your mind.

# GOLFER'S JOURNAL

www.ingramcontent.com/pod-product-compliance
Lightning Source LLC
Chambersburg PA
CBHW050037040726
47599CB00015B/1715